ONE VERSE EVANGELISM®

(A SIMPLE WAY TO SHARE THE GOSPEL)

NAVPRESS®

NavPress is the publishing ministry of The Navigators, an international Christian organization and leader in personal spiritual development. NavPress is committed to helping people grow spiritually and enjoy lives of meaning and hope through personal and group resources that are biblically rooted, culturally relevant, and highly practical.

For more information, visit www.NavPress.com.

One-Verse Evangelism

A NavPress resource published in alliance with Tyndale House Publishers, Inc.

Design by Steve Learned

ISBN 978-0-9729023-6-6

Printed in the United States of America

25 24 23
10 9 8 7 6

For the wages of sin is death, but the gift of God is eternal life in Christ Jesus our Lord.

— Romans 6:23

Love is simple.

God has reached out to the world with a love that is beautiful, sacrificial, and invitational, yet at the same time very simple. *Anyone* can experience it, and *anyone* who has experienced it can share that good news with others.

Would we talk about God's love more openly with others if we had a clear and simple way to do it? Here is one way that I have found to converse our faith naturally and authentically. To do this, we must first understand ourselves, people, and the gospel.

Self

God has chosen us, imperfect humans, to share His perfect love. We don't have to be perfect to point others to Him. We just need to be authentic about ourselves and honest about the gospel.

When Paul spoke of his faith, he was honest enough to admit his own struggles. He said he was "hard pressed on every side, but not crushed; perplexed, but not in despair; persecuted, but not abandoned; struck down, but not destroyed" (2 Corinthians 4:8–10). These verses encourage me because they allow me to be real about my own inadequacies. I used to think that people were more drawn to Christ if my life was in order and free of problems. Now I realize that people are drawn to Christ when they see me hard pressed—even perplexed—yet honest about it. I can now admit that often I feel weak and need to draw strength from someone outside of myself: God.

Authenticity is more influential than perfection.

People

No two people are the same. In the Bible, when people share Christ's message, they do it with variety and creativity. In the Scriptures, we don't often see the gospel shared in the same format or with the same words.

Before telling others about Christ's love, we should try to understand who they are. God wants His love shared in a way that makes sense to the listener. To do that, we must study people as Jesus did and understand how each person is different. We never have to change the truth to fit the individual, but we should seek ways to explain Christ's love in light of a person's background and personality. "To the weak I became weak, to win the weak. I have become all things to all men so that by all possible means I might save some" (1 Corinthians 9:22).

Love is adaptable.

Gospel

The gospel is about God's love *and our response to it*. We don't need to make it any more complicated than that. While it is deep, it's also simple. When we explain to others how to accept that love, we should follow Paul's advice to "proclaim it clearly" (Colossians 4:4). So how can we do that?

You can start a conversation in a number of ways. You can ask, "Have you ever wondered why you are here on earth? There's a short sentence in the Bible that has helped me answer that question. Would you like to see it?" Or, "Has anyone explained the meaning of the Bible to you in one simple picture? If you are interested, I can draw it for you."

1

Copy Romans 6:23 onto the top of a piece of paper.

2

Draw a person.

3

Underline the word "wages" and write it underneath the person.

4

Draw a down arrow under "wages."

For the wages of sin is death, but the gif

The one-verse illustration

If you have memorized Romans 6:23, write the verse on top of a piece of blank paper (or a napkin or whatever is handy). If you prefer to open up your Bible, turn to the verse in Romans and copy it onto the top of a piece of paper. Then close your Bible and set it aside. On the left side of the paper draw a simple picture of a person.

"God is very creative. He's never made two people exactly alike, so it is only natural that each of us responds to Him in a different way."

wages

Underline the word *wages* at the top of the page, then write it underneath the person.

"How would you explain what wages are?" (Wages are what you receive in exchange for what you have done.) "Have you ever had a job where you earned wages?" (Follow up with one or two questions about the job.) "How would you feel if one day your employer refused to give you the wages that you earned?"

"We all know it is only right that a person gets what he has earned. God says that we also have earned certain wages."

Draw a downward arrow under *wages*.

5

Underline the word "sin," then write it underneath "wages."

6

Draw a downward arrow from "wages" to "sin."

7

Write the word "God" across from the person.

8

Add the cliffs.

9

Draw a downward arrow under "sin."

For the wages of sin is death, but the gif

sin

Underline the word *sin* at the top of the page, and write it underneath the word *wages* on the left side of the page.

"There are wages that come with sin. What do you think of when you hear the word, 'sin'"?

Write the word *God* on the right side of the paper across from the person.

"Sin is an attitude more than an action. Some of us actively rebel against God. Others are apathetic and just leave Him out of their lives. Either way, we are pushing God away."

Draw a cliff on the left side underneath the person and over the words *wages* and *sin*. Add another cliff on the right side under the word *God*. Point to the distance between the person and God.

"The distance between God and us is the same distance that is created between any two people when one hurts or disregards the other. That's what sin does between God and us. God seems distant because we selfishly choose to focus on ourselves instead of Him."

Draw a downward arrow under *sin*.

"What sin does is represented by the next key word, *death*."

is eternal life in Christ Jesus our Lord. —Romans 6:23

10

Underline the word “death,” then write it underneath “sin.”

11

Draw a circle several times around the word “death.”

12

Add the word “HELP” under the word “death,” and draw a slash through it.

13

Add the word “HOPE” under the word “death,” and draw a slash through it.

death

Underline the word *death* on the top of the page, and write it underneath the word *sin*.

"Death in the Bible always means separation. When we are dead to God, we are separated from Him; we have no life or relationship with Him.

"When we separate ourselves from God, it bothers Him. Actually, it hurts Him because He wants a loving relationship with us."

Draw a circle several times around the word *death*, while explaining:

"If we go through life separated from God, we remain alone, terrifyingly alone."

Draw the word *help* below and to the left outside the circle.

"When problems come up in life and we need help, we can't go to God if we are separated from Him, either now or in the future."

Draw a slash through *help*.

Draw the word *hope* below and to the right of the circle.

"And when we are trying to find hope for our lives, we're left to ourselves—often hopeless."

As you say this, draw a slash through *hope*.

is eternal life in Christ Jesus our Lord. —Romans 6:23

14

Underline the word "but," then write it between the cliffs.

For the wages of sin is death, but the gift of God is eternal life in Christ Jesus our Lord.

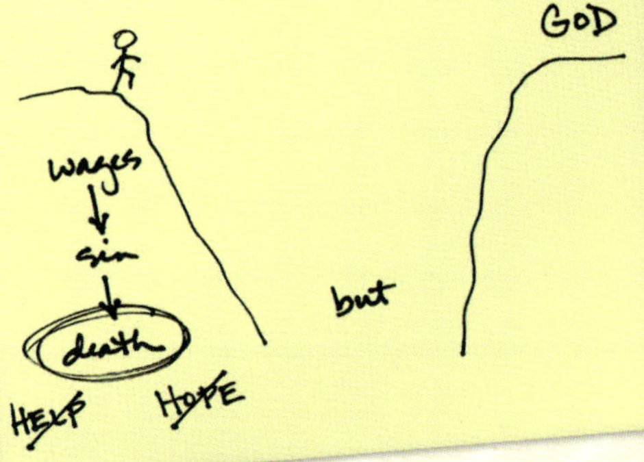

For the wages of sin is death, but the

but

Underline the word *but* on the top of the page, and write it at the bottom between the cliffs.

This one simple word signals that everything you just explained is about to be contrasted.

"What we just looked at is the bad news (pointing to the cliff on the left). Now let's take a look at the good news (pointing to the cliff on the right)."

is eternal life in Christ Jesus our Lord. —Romans 6:23

15

Underline the word "gift," then write it under the right cliff.

16

Draw a downward arrow under "gift."

gift

For the wages of sin is death, but the gift of God is eternal life in Christ Jesus our Lord.

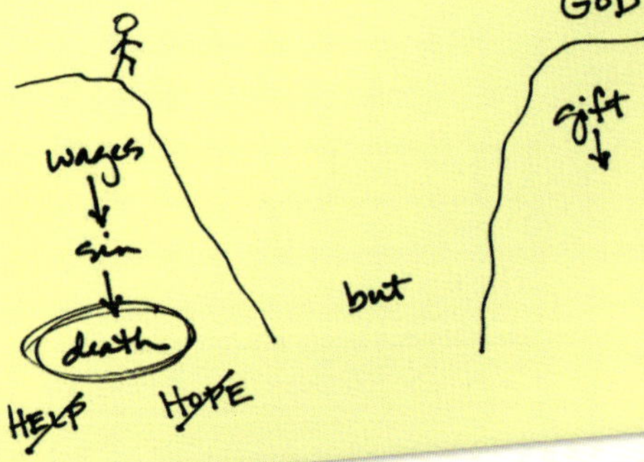

For the wages of sin is death, but the gif

gift

Underline the word *gift* at the top of the page, and write it in under the right cliff.

"Now, let's look at the opposites. If wages (pointing to *wages*) are something we earn, then (pointing to *gift*) what is a gift?" (A gift is something that is not earned; it is given freely.)

"Imagine that a friend of yours offered you a gift. Instead of receiving it gratefully, you demanded to pay your friend the cost of the gift. How do you think he would feel? God feels the same way when He offers us the gift of His love. We cannot pay for it. He hopes we accept it."

Draw a downward arrow under *gift*.

is eternal life in Christ Jesus our Lord. —Romans 6:23

17

Underline the word "God," then write it under "gift."

18

Draw a downward arrow under "God."

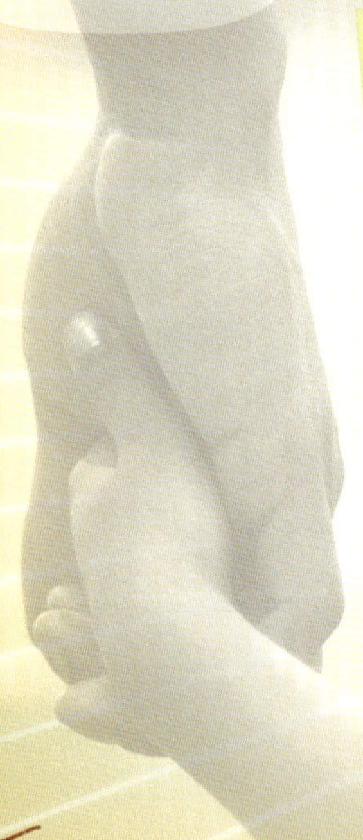

For the wages of sin is death, but the gift of God is eternal life in Christ Jesus our Lord.

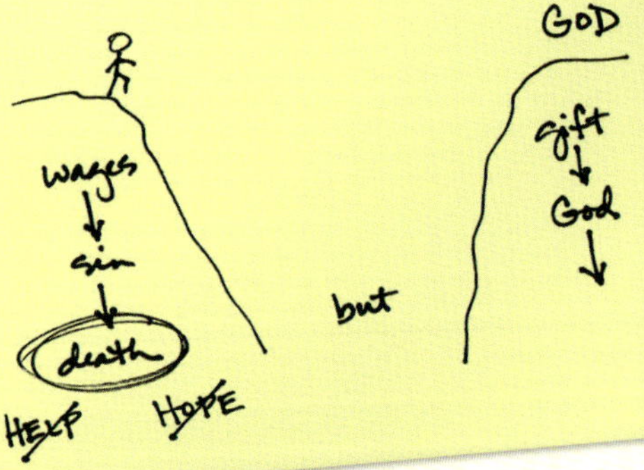

For the wages of sin is death, but the gif

God

Underline the word *God* in the verse, and write it on the right cliff under *gift*. Draw a downward arrow under *gift*.

"This gift is from God."

"Remember that sin (point to *sin*) is leaving God out of our lives, either intentionally or by just ignoring Him. It is living without God and instead being selfishly consumed with ourselves. God is the exact opposite (point to the word *God* on the right cliff). He is selfless. He loves us."

Draw a downward arrow under *God*.

"The gift He offers is unlike any other gift."

is eternal life in Christ Jesus our Lord. —Romans 6:23

19

Underline the words "eternal life," then write them underneath "God."

20

Draw a circle several times around the words "eternal life."

21

Add the word "HELP" under the words "eternal life."

22

Add the word "HOPE" under the words "eternal life."

For the wages of sin is death, but the gif

eternal life

Underline the words *eternal life* in the verse, and write these words on the right cliff under *God.*

"Eternal life is the opposite of death (point to the left cliff). If death is separation from God, then what is eternal life?" (A relationship, a closeness with Him.) "Because God made us, He wants to have a lasting friendship with us. This friendship starts now and lasts forever. It's an amazing thought, but He really likes us and wants to spend time with us. If we go through life in a relationship with God (draw a circle several times around *eternal life*), we are never alone—ever. (Draw the word *help* outside the circle, below and to the left.) Now God helps us and gives us His strength."

Draw the word *hope* across from the word *help.*

"We also have hope for the future because He will never leave us. But how do we receive this gift?"

is eternal life in Christ Jesus our Lord. —Romans 6:23

23

Underline "Christ Jesus."

24

Add a cross bridging the gap between the two cliffs.

25

Add the words "Jesus Christ" to the cross.

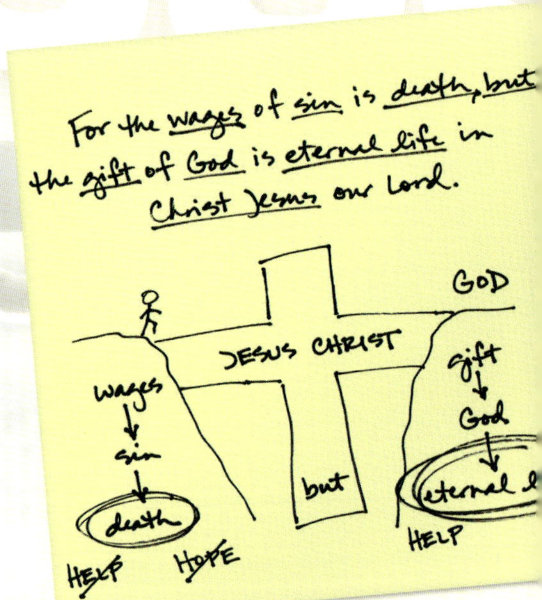

For the wages of sin is death, but the gif

Jesus Christ

Underline the words *Christ Jesus* at the top of the page, and draw a cross between the cliffs as a bridge, writing the words *Jesus Christ* (or *Christ Jesus*) inside.

"Jesus Christ is the source of eternal life. When a person chooses to sin, there are wages—death—that go with that sin (point to the left side of the cliff). Someone—either you or Jesus—must pay that penalty. We get to decide who it will be; it is entirely up to us. Jesus died in your place so you wouldn't have to, but He never forces Himself on anyone. He offers us forgiveness if we will ask for it from our hearts."

is eternal life in Christ Jesus our Lord. —Romans 6:23

26

Add the word "believe" across the top of the cross.

27

Draw an arrow through "believe" showing the motion of the person going to God.

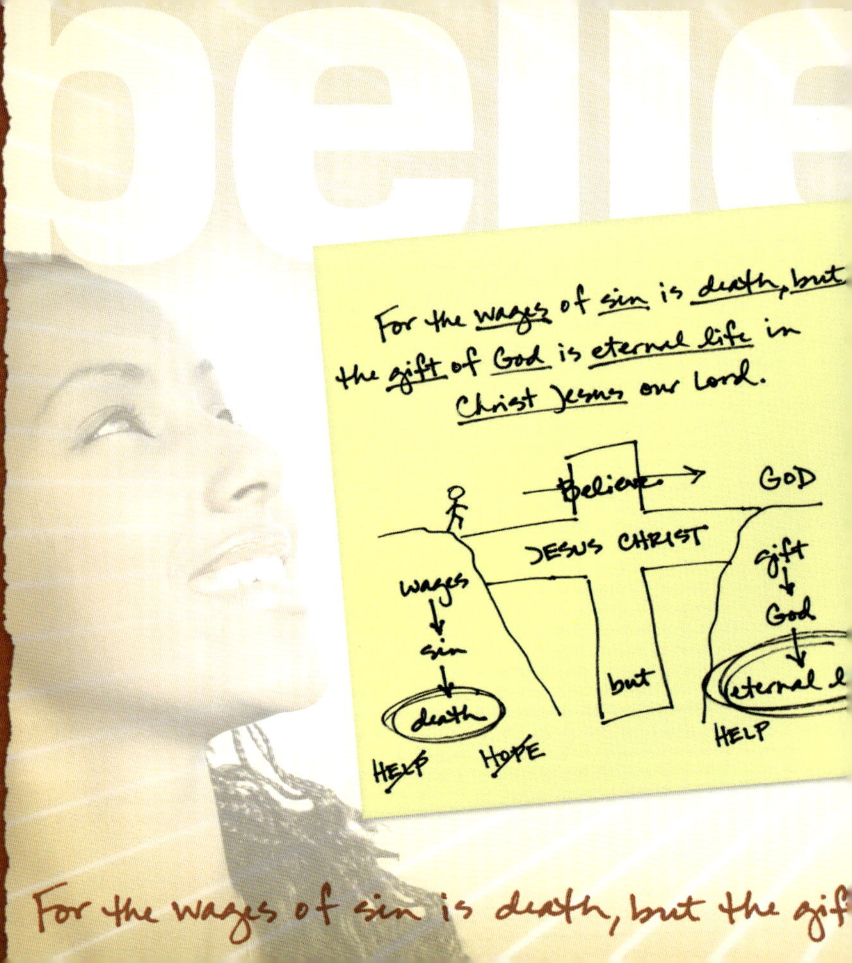

believe

Write the word *believe* across the top of the cross.

"If we accept the fact that we have been selfish and have sinned, we can ask Jesus to forgive us. When we ask Jesus to forgive our sins, we cross over the bridge from death to eternal life. It starts instantly and lasts forever.

"We have a choice. We can be friends with God and receive the help and hope He offers, or we can try to live without him.

"As you look at this illustration, what do we need to do to have eternal life and a friendship with God?" (If the person does not understand any part of the illustration, go back and answer any questions.)

"Is there anything that would keep you from believing in Jesus Christ and beginning that relationship?"

If the person is ready to make that decision, help him ask God for forgiveness, but give him the freedom to use his own words if he wants to.

is eternal life in Christ Jesus our Lord. —Romans 6:23